MICROSOFT 2016 2013 WORD 2010 2007

TIPS, *Tricks* AND SHORTCUTS

PLUS LINKS TO TRAINING VIDEOS!

35 MINI-LESSONS TO WORK SMARTER, SAVE TIME, AND INCREASE PRODUCTIVITY

SECOND EDITION

BLACK & WHITE VERSION

by

Amelia Griggs

Table of Contents

About This Book

HOW TO USE THIS BOOK

Although you are welcome to follow this book from beginning to end, feel free to browse through the table of contents to select specific shortcuts that you want to learn right away. Since it's packed with lots of tips, tricks, and even some secrets, you can pick and choose the features that are right for you. The intention of this book and its contents is to make your life easier by providing quick and easy-to-follow instructions designed to help you work smarter, save time and increase productivity.

If you are new to Microsoft Word, please see the "For Beginners Only" topics #1 through 5, for a quick and easy review of the basics of Microsoft Word. Topics 6 through 35 cover intermediate features and a few advanced techniques.

WHAT'S INCLUDED IN THIS BOOK

This book contains 35 mini-lessons including step-by-step instructions, packed with a wide collection of tips, tricks and shortcuts that I've been collecting for many years for use with Microsoft Word. Some shortcuts have been around since the early versions of Microsoft Word, while others have been added as "new" features in later versions of Microsoft Word.

Most people only take advantage of less than half of all features in software. Why? Most of us are under pressure to get work done as quickly as possible, so there's rarely enough time in a day to figure out all the time-saving shortcuts in a software program. Instead, we either keep doing what we *think* is the best way to do something, or we might reach out to a co-worker to see if he or she knows a faster way to accomplish a task.

In today's fast-paced world, gone are the days where we have the time and energy to sit through hours and hours of software training, only to learn that by the end of the day, we only remember a small portion of what was covered. In most cases, unless we practice what we have learned in the days following, a large portion of what the instructor shows us in several hours is forgotten in as little as 1 to 2 weeks. This is because of the "use it or lose it" principle. The best way to retain knowledge is to practice it and re-use it frequently. Otherwise, it is sure to be forgotten.

"I hear and I forget. I see and I remember. I do and I understand."

~ Confucius

BITE SIZED LEARNING

What we really need are quick little lessons, or "bursts" of knowledge to take in with ease. It's just like eating a meal. Sitting down to a heavy meal is harder to digest as compared to smaller meals. It's the same with learning. If you take too much in at once, you run the risk of experiencing cognitive overload.

Short lessons or "bite-sized learning" modules allow us to absorb small amounts of meaningful information in a brief amount of time. Also, you can pick and choose to learn only what interests you.

WHAT VERSIONS OF WORD DOES THIS BOOK APPLY TO?

All instructions and shortcuts in this book have been tested in Word 2016, 2013, 2010 and 2007. Word 2016 is shown in most of the screen prints in this book. If there are any major differences between versions, it is noted throughout the book.

I hope you find the content in this book very helpful!

BONUS! Companion Videos

For each of the 35 sections in this book, there is a companion training video. You can search for each video using the corresponding hashtag. Here's how:

1. Navigate to www.youtube.com
2. In the search box, enter the hashtag search word provided at the end of each section (remember to include "#") which is #ezword+[the video number]. For example:
   > To locate video #1, search for: *#ezword1*
   > To locate video #2, search for: *#ezword2*
   > ...and so forth...
   > To locate video #35, search for: *#ezword35*
3. Click Search (the magnifying glass icon).

Here's an example of the results:

Each video contains demonstrations of all the instructions included in each section in this book, plus some additional information. Be sure to check out each training video to see the steps in action and learn even more!

To see all available training videos, visit the Easy Learning YouTube channel at: www.youtube.com/user/easylearningweb or scan the image below:

From the Easy Learning channel, click "PLAYLISTS" to see training videos grouped by topic. See the PLAYLIST entitled "Microsoft Word How-To Videos" to see all Microsoft Word training videos.

Part I: For Beginners Only

Contents

For Beginners Only

What's This Thing Called Word?

What Can Microsoft Word Be Used For?

Quick and Simple Formatting

Opening, Saving, and Closing Documents

Previewing and Printing Documents

#1: What's This Thing Called Word?

Microsoft Word is a powerful word processor that allows you to create, edit, and print anything from simple memos to complex forms. Let's compare Word to some more basic editing tools.

Some very *simple* word processing can be accomplished in the Windows accessory, Notepad. But for most of us, Notepad is just that: a little pad for notes. However, Notepad can come in handy if you need a "no frills" text editor with no formatting.

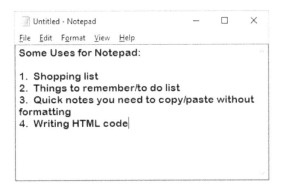

A step up from Notepad is WordPad. Whether or not you've heard of WordPad, it's been there all this time. WordPad is like a baby version of Word. WordPad looks a lot like Word, but with very limited capabilities. In earlier versions of Windows, WordPad can be found in Accessories under Programs. Starting with Windows 10, WordPad can be found by clicking in Windows Accessories under All Apps.

And then there's Microsoft Word, which is the mother of all Word Processors. It contains a plethora of advanced features, some of which you may never need. This includes columns, tables, templates, headers, footers, SmartArt, hyperlinks, text boxes, footnotes, endnotes, labels, mail merge, citations, bibliographies, table of contents, and a whole lot more. Microsoft Word is one of the various applications under the Microsoft Office umbrella suite of powerful software programs.

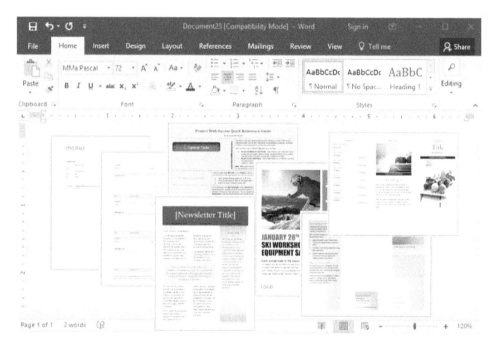

View Companion Video #1 to see these steps in action

Go to www.youtube.com and search for *#ezword1*

#2:What Can Microsoft Word Be Used For?

Microsoft Word can be used for practically any type of document that you can think of, from something as simple as a one-page letter, to something more complex, like a company newsletter – chock full of graphics, colors, fancy text, and hyperlinks. You don't have to start from scratch. Gone are the days when you had to start with blank sheets of white paper on a typewriter. Microsoft Word makes it easy for you by providing a variety of pre-formatted templates. You can even create your own custom templates. Here are just a few examples of what you can create in Microsoft Word:

Business letter   Business plan   Business Flyer   Newsletter

Purchase order   Work order   Packing slip (Simple Lin...   Project status report (Re...

Tri-fold brochure (blue)   Project-based learning rubric   Project management quick reference

There are literally thousands of templates available. To get started, click File, New, and then enter a search term in the search box, or click on a category and view templates for Business, Personal, Design Sets, Event, Education or Labels.

Once you select a template, customize and edit as needed, then use File, Save As to save a copy. To save a customized template or a new document that you created as a template to reuse easily in the future, click File, Save As, and select Word Template (*.dotx) as the file type. It's as easy as that!

View Companion Video #2 to see these steps in action

Go to www.youtube.com and search for **#ezword2**

#3: Quick and Simple Formatting

To apply simple formatting (including font, font size, font color, bold, italics, underline, etc.):

1. Select the text to be formatted. *Did you know you can use your mouse as well as your keyboard to select your text?*
   - **Select with mouse**: Point your mouse and drag to highlight (select) text.
   - **Select with keyboard**: Hold SHIFT and use an arrow key to highlight (select) text.

2. Once the text to be formatted is selected, from the Home tab in the Ribbon, click on the desired icon in the Font group:

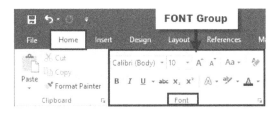

Some icons in the Font Group have drop-down arrows. Hover over a drop-down arrow to view a tool tip to identify the function. Click the drop-down arrow to view menu choices to select from:

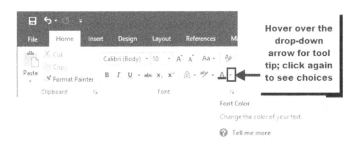

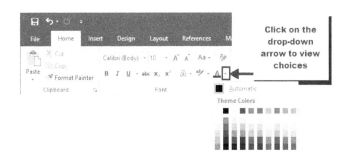

After selecting text, while hovering over the selected text, a shortcut font menu (shown at the top of the image below), displays for you. It includes font group icons as well as some paragraph formatting icons. The font shortcut menu disappears once you move the mouse away from the selected text. You can bring the shortcut menu back by right clicking on your selected text. Doing so displays yet another menu, with even more options. Need more formatting features? Click on "Font…" (that's the word "Font" with the ellipses after it) in the right-click menu to display the full Font dialog box.

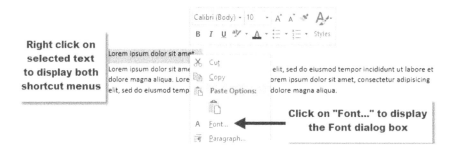

View Companion Video #3 to see these steps in action

Go to www.youtube.com and search for **#ezword3**

#4: Opening, Saving, and Closing Documents

Opening, saving, and closing documents are easy to do, but newer versions of Microsoft Word, like Word 2016, offers even more choices when executing these commands.

The good old-fashioned way to open, save, or close a document is to click File, then click the appropriate command from the File menu. If you've ever used Office 2007, you might have noticed that the File command was removed and replaced with a circular image called the Office button, which looked like this:

Luckily, in Office 2010 and beyond, File is back!

In Office 2013/2016, the File menu has been updated a bit. The Open/Save As commands now display in the right panel, including options to open or save on OneDrive. Take a look:

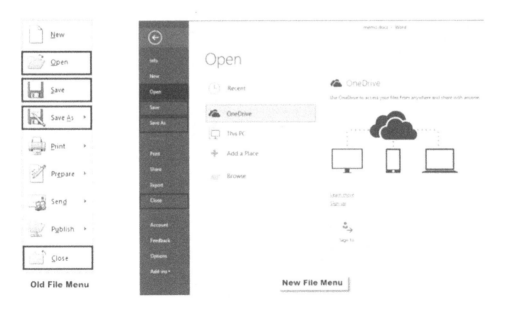

The new File menu in Word 2016 has some additional options including "Info" (for Document Properties, Conversion and Protection options), "Share" (for easy ways to share with others via email, blog or online), "Export" (to create PDF/XPS documents and other file types), "Account" (for accessing your Microsoft account options), "Feedback" (to provide feedback to Microsoft), "Options" (originally the Word Options button, for setup of global options) and "Add-ins" (for additional Add-ins installed in your version).

Let's get back to the Open, Save and Close commands. Other than the File menu, another way to execute these commands is via keyboard shortcuts:

- CTRL+O = Open
- CTRL+S = Save
- CTRL+W = Save and Close (this option saves and then immediately closes your document)

View Companion Video #4 to see these steps in action

Go to www.youtube.com and search for **#ezword4**

#5:Previewing and Printing Documents

To print a document, click File, Print, or use the keyboard shortcut, CTRL+P.

The Print dialog box in Word 2013/2016 includes several new menu items:

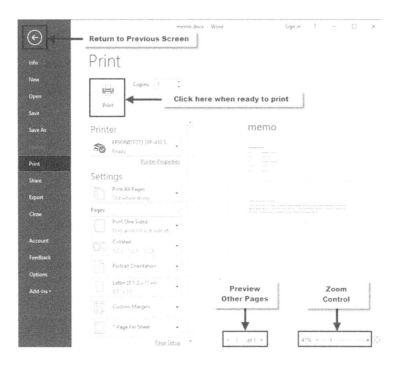

Note: In older versions of Word, it was necessary to click File, Print, Print Preview, to preview a document. In newer versions of Word (2013/2016), the preview of the document is automatically included on the right side of the Print dialog box, as seen in the image above.

View Companion Video #5 to see these steps in action

Go to www.youtube.com and search for *#ezword5*

Part II: *Typing and Formatting*

Contents

Typing and Formatting

#6: Click and Type in the Middle of the Page

Let's say you need to make a sign that says "Meeting in Progress" and you want the text centered, about halfway down the page.

You may be tempted to press the Enter key about a dozen or so times to try to figure out where the middle of the page is located.

Did you know there is an easier way?

Just use the Click and Type feature!

In a new document window, simply double-click at any point in the document and begin typing.

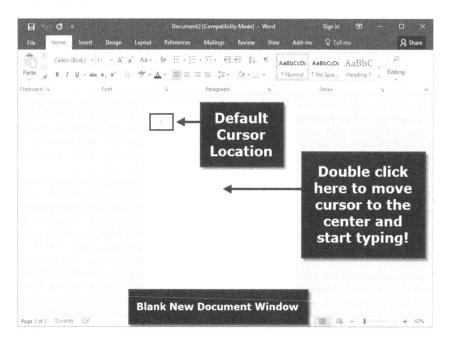

With a quick adjustment of font size, you can create a quick sign in no time!

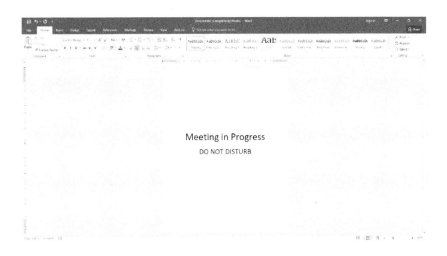

Meeting in Progress
DO NOT DISTURB

View Companion Video #6 to see these steps in action

Go to www.youtube.com and search for *#ezword6*

#7: Adjust Line Spacing in a Snap

To quickly change the line spacing for a paragraph using the keyboard:

1. Position the cursor anywhere in the paragraph you would like to modify.
2. Then, press one of the following:
   - Ctrl+1 for single spacing
   - Ctrl+2 for double spacing
   - Ctrl+5 for 1 ½ line spacing

Another way to change line spacing is to:

1. Right click in the paragraph (or for multiple paragraphs, select a larger area of text, and then right click).
2. Click "Paragraph…"
3. The Paragraph dialog box displays. Click the drop-down arrow under Line spacing and click to select the line spacing option.
4. Click OK.

From the Ribbon, you can also access the Paragraph dialog box by clicking on the diagonal arrow on the bottom right of the Paragraph group.

View Companion Video #7 to see these steps in action

Go to www.youtube.com and search for **#ezword7**

#8: Turning Off Auto Format and Auto Correct

Do you have a love/hate relationship with Auto Correct? Word is merely trying to help when it attempts to correct a possible misspelling, or to add a number or bullet when it thinks you're typing a list. You don't have to live with all Auto Correction options; you can decide what options work best for you.

To access Auto Correct options, click File, Options (Word Options in Word 2007), Proofing, AutoCorrect Options:

From the AutoCorrect dialog box, click on each of the tabs to view all options as shown below. There are a multitude of options to consider. Uncheck a box to turn the feature off, or check the box to turn on, and then click OK.

Here are some tips for some of the handier Auto Correct options to consider changing or experimenting with:

Replace Text As You Type:

On the AutoCorrect dialog box, the **Replace text as you type** option can come in handy to set up shortcuts and cut down on edits and typing. For example, if there is a long name like Nathaniel Rosenbloomburg, you can add a replacement command so that when you type nr, the full name will fill in automatically:

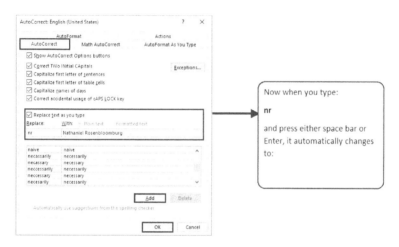

Change Style of Quotes:

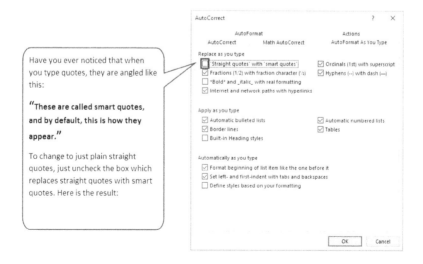

Turning Off Auto Numbering or Auto Bullet Lists:

If Word thinks you're typing a numbered list or a bulleted list, it attempts to format the list for you.

To turn off automatic numbered or bulleted lists, in the AutoFormat "As You Type" tab, deselect the "Automatic bulleted lists" or "Automatic numbered lists" checkbox, and you're back in control of exactly when you want to insert a bulleted or numbered list.

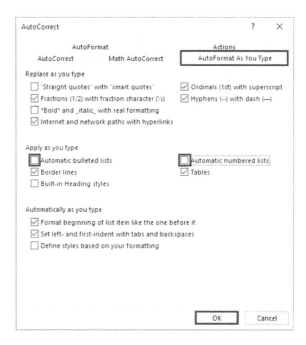

To Get More Help With AutoCorrect Options:

Since there are more than enough options in AutoCorrect for one to quickly understand, to learn more about the many AutoCorrect options, with the AutoCorrect dialog box open, click on the question mark to learn more about AutoCorrect features:

View Companion Video #8 to see these steps in action

Go to www.youtube.com and search for **ezword8**

Have you ever forgotten to capitalize the words in a title? Or have you finished creating a document only to have it returned with edits requiring you to change certain words to initial caps instead of all caps, or vice versa?

Picture this: Your manager has just finished reviewing an important business document that she needs you to edit for a meeting that is taking place in 20 minutes. She has several edits including changing several proper names to ALL CAPS, and changing all page titles to lower case. Search and replace won't necessarily save you time because all the names to be changed are different. There are approximately 20 page titles. There's absolutely no time to retype the text, and even if there was time, retyping text will increase the likelihood that errors will occur. You need a quick way to change the case in a jiffy! ***What do you do?***

There are a couple ways to quickly change the case and toggle between ALL CAPS, Initial Caps, or all lower case.

Fastest Option to Change Case:

1. Select the word, sentence, or phrase you want to modify.
2. Hold the SHIFT key down and then tap F3 as many times as needed to scroll through the available cases, including ALL CAPS, initial caps or lower case.

Give it try! Type a few words, and select the text. Then press SHIFT + F3 and watch the text case change!

Another Way to Change Case Using the Ribbon:

1. Select the word, sentence, or paragraph you want to modify.
2. From the Home tab on the Ribbon, click the Change Case icon.
3. From the list of Change Case options, select the desired option:

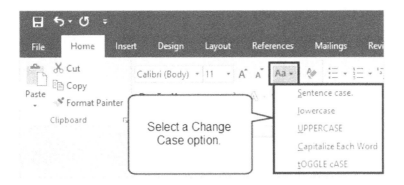

View Companion Video #9 to see these steps in action

Go to www.youtube.com and search for ***#ezword9***

#10:   A Non-Breaking Space Will Keep It Together

If you need to keep words together, such as a proper name or a hyphenated word, so that they are not separated on another line, you can use Word's non-breaking space, or non-breaking hyphen. *Here's how:*

To keep words together using a non-breaking space:

1. Type your first word. For example, type: **John** (then don't press the spacebar).
2. Press Ctrl + Shift + Spacebar (to insert a non-breaking space).
3. Type your second word. For example, type: **Smith**.

Voila! Now the words will never separate on another line.

To keep hyphenated words together using a non-breaking hyphen:

1. Type your first word. For example, type: **well** (then don't press the spacebar).
2. Press Ctrl + Shift + Hyphen (to insert a non-breaking hyphen).
3. Type your second word. For example, type: **being**.

Non-breaking hyphens prevent hyphenated words, numbers, or phrases from breaking if they fall at the end of a line of text. So, in this example, you can prevent **well-being** from breaking; instead, it will always remain together and never separate.

View Companion Video #10 to see these steps in action

Go to www.youtube.com and search for ***#ezword10***

#11:   *Text Selection Tricks*

Do you select text with your mouse by pointing and dragging? Did you know there are lots of other ways to select text?

Selecting Words and Paragraphs Using Your Mouse:

- To select one word, double-click while pointing to the word with your mouse.
- To select a paragraph, triple-click while pointing anywhere in the paragraph.
- To select the entire document, position your mouse in the left margin of your document and triple click.

Selecting Text Using Your Keyboard:

- To select text left to right, click on the starting point, then press Shift+right arrow to select text.
- To select right to left, click on the starting point, then press Shift+left arrow to select text.
- To select the entire document, press CTRL+A (Select All).

Did You Know You Can Also Select a Rectangular Area of Text? Here's how:

- Position the mouse pointer at the beginning position of the selection.
- Hold the ALT key down while you drag. That's it! See an example in the image below.

Client will be invoiced all costs associated with out-of-pocket expenses (including, without limitation, costs and expenses associated with meals, lodging, local transportation and any other applicable business expenses) listed on the invoice as a separate line item. Reimbursement for out-of-pocket expenses in connection with performance of this SOW, when authorized and up to the limits set forth in this SOW, shall be in accordance with Client's then-current published policies governing travel and associated business expenses, which information shall be provided by the Client Project Manager. The limit of reimbursable expenses pursuant to this SOW is estimated to be 15% of the fees unless otherwise authorized in writing and agreed to by both parties via the project change control procedure outlined within.

This can come in handy if you have a document set up with tabbed columns and you need to change the formatting of that particular portion of your list. In the example below, the title and text in the second column were selected; then italics and font color changes were applied:

Project ID	Company	POC	Beginning Date	End Date
P100	ABC Corp	John Smith	01/10/17	2/20/17
P101	XYZ Inc	Mary Jones	01/15/17	3/1/17
P103	New Age Corp	Ann Meyer	02/1/17	4/10/17

Project ID	Company	POC	Beginning Date	End Date
P100	*ABC Corp*	John Smith	01/10/17	2/20/17
P101	*XYZ Inc*	Mary Jones	01/15/17	3/1/17
P103	*New Age Corp*	Ann Meyer	02/1/17	4/10/17

View Companion Video #11 to see these steps in action

Go to www.youtube.com and search for *#ezword11*

#12:   *Saving Steps Using the Format Painter*

What is the Format Painter?

The Format Painter, which is the little paint brush icon on the Home tab, allows you to quickly apply the same formatting such as color, font size, image edge effect, etc. from one area of your document to another. This includes both text and graphic formatting.

You can use the Format Painter for simple changes, like applying bold and italics to selective words or phrases throughout your document, or for more complex changes, like applying border edge effects to various images throughout your document. The Format Painter can save a tremendous amount of time. In addition, it can help your document retain consistent style and formatting.

To use the Format Painter:

1. Click on the text or object which contains the formatting you would like to copy.

2. Click the Format Painter icon   . You will then notice a little paintbrush displays next to your mouse pointer (I-beam) which looks like this: .

3. Position your mouse pointer (which shows the little paintbrush symbol) to the text or graphic to apply the formatting, and then either click to apply the formatting to one word or one object, or click and drag to *paint* over a large area of text or objects to apply formatting.

Note: To use the format painter multiple times in your document, double-click the Format Painter icon in #1 above. The little paint brush which displays next to your mouse pointer will remain so that you can apply formatting to additional areas of your document. Then press the Esc key when finished.

Still not convinced that the Format Painter is your best friend?

Consider these scenarios for when the Format Painter can save the day:

Scenario #1:

- You just formatted a lengthy document which contains 20 numbered lists on various pages. Instead of numbered lists, you need to change to bulleted lists. ***What do you do?***
    - **Option 1**: Select each numbered list, then click the bullet icon (40 steps).
    - **Option 2**: Select only the first numbered list, click the bullet icon, double-click the Format Painter icon; then swipe over each of the 19 remaining numbered lists to change each to a bulleted list (22 steps). ***The Format Painter saves 18 steps!***

Scenario #2:

- You have submitted a report to your manager, and he needs a few edits done as soon as possible for a meeting which will begin in 30 minutes. He also needs 50 copies printed. He hands you the printed report and has circled certain words throughout the report; he asks that the circled words be italicized, bolded, and highlighted in yellow. You rush back to your desk and get started. You look over the pages and count 28 words that your manager highlighted. You need to come up with the fastest way to accomplish this task. ***What do you do?***
    - **Option 1**: Use your mouse to select each word; then from the Ribbon, click Bold, click Italics, then click the yellow highlight icon. This is 4 steps per word (112 steps).
    - **Option 2**: Apply the formatting to the first word only, double-click the Format Painter icon, and click on each of the other words to apply the formatting. For example:
        - First, select the word; from the Ribbon, click Bold, click Italics, then click on the yellow highlight icon (4 steps so far). Then double-click the Format Painter icon (5 steps so far). Next, click on each of the other words to apply the same formatting (27 other words, so 27 more clicks). Finally, press ESC when finished to turn off the Format Painter. Total steps: 32. ***The Format Painter saves 80 steps!***

Scenario #3:

- You are on a committee at your daughter's school and you created a draft of a booklet for an upcoming book fair fundraiser. The booklet is filled with pictures of students as well as thumbnails of book covers (24 images in all). The committee has requested that a border be added to all the images (1.5" blue border with shadow effect). They would like the change made to all the photos by the next day to send to the printer. ***What's the fastest way to accomplish this?***
    - o **Option 1**: Right click on the first image, select Format Picture, click Line Color, Solid Line; click Line Style and change width to 1.5pt; click Shadow/click on Shadow effect, click Close (approximately 12 steps to format one image). Repeat all steps for each image (approximately 288 clicks).
    - o **Option 2**: Apply the desired border effect to the first image only (same steps above, approximately 12 steps to format one image). Next, double-click the Format Painter icon; then click on each of the other images; finally, press ESC to turn off the Format Painter. Total steps: 36. ***The Format Painter saves 252 steps!***
        - ▪ **Note**: In this example, if the images are next to each other with no text in between, instead of clicking on each image, you can swipe, or *paint* the entire area containing multiple images to apply the border effect to all images at once, thereby saving even more time!

View Companion Video #12 to see these steps in action

Go to www.youtube.com and search for ***#ezword12***

When you place a header or footer in a Word document, by default, the header or footer is applied to the entire document. One exception is if you click on either the Different First Page or the Different Odd & Even Pages option in the Ribbon. When you double click in the header (or footer) area in your document, the Ribbon automatically displays the Header and Footer Tools Ribbon as shown below.

Different First Page allows you to create a unique header and footer on page 1. Then the header/footer you setup on page 2 carries over onto all remaining pages.

Different Odd & Even Pages allows you to create one header/footer for all even pages, and a second header/footer for all odd pages.

If you need even more unique headers and footers on other pages, you can insert **Section Breaks**. This will allow you to create a different header and footer for each section. *Here's how*:

1. Open a blank Word document.
2. Double-click on the header area. Insert something into the header (for example: "Header #1").
3. Double-click in the body of page 1 (below the header area).
4. Press CTRL+ENTER to enter a page break. Now you should have 2 pages with the same header.
5. Press CTRL+ENTER to enter a page break. Now you should have 3 pages with the same header. On page 3, type "This is the first section".
6. Next, on page 3, click Layout; then click on the drop-down menu next to Break. Under Section Breaks, select Next Page.

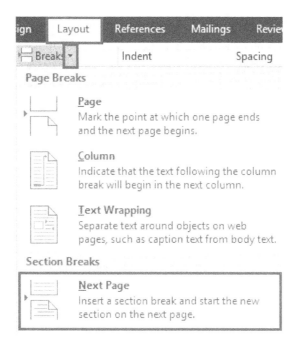

7. To confirm that your Section Break was inserted, click Show Hide. If you haven't used Show/Hide, it is a very helpful tool that shows paragraph marks and other hidden formatting symbols. You should then see the Section Break clearly marked, as shown below.

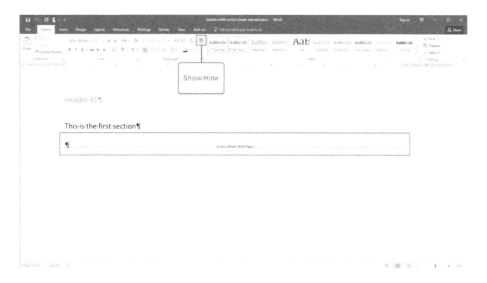

8. Next, scroll down to page 4, which will have the same header as earlier pages. Double-click in the header area. Notice the notation "Same as Previous" on the far right. The same header will carry over into new sections unless you do one more ***important*** step. On the Ribbon, click Link to Previous to toggle this feature off. Turning this feature off will allow you to create a different header (or footer) for the current section. Finally, change the header on page 4 to "Header #2." Your document should match with the image below:

That's it! Now if you scroll up to page 3 and earlier pages, the "Header #1" remains the same for that section (your first section) of your document. The second section (which starts on page 4) now has a unique header. You can set up a unique footer in the same manner.

View Companion Video #13 to see these steps in action

Go to www.youtube.com and search for ***#ezword13***

#14:   *Creating/Inserting a Table of Contents*

In order to create a table of contents, all you have to do is apply Heading styles to the text you want to include in the table of contents. For example, let's say you've typed the first section of a report which includes an Introduction. To include *Section I* in the first level of the Table of Contents, select the text *Section I* and then click Heading 1:

To include *Introduction* in the second level of the Table of Contents, select the word *Introduction* and then click Heading 2:

Once you have applied Heading styles to your text, to insert a table of contents:

1. Move to the page in the document where you would like to insert the table of contents.
2. From the References tab on the Ribbon, click Table of Contents.
3. Select an Automatic Table of Contents style from the list. In this example, Automatic Table 2 style is selected.
4. The Table of Contents is then inserted in your document.

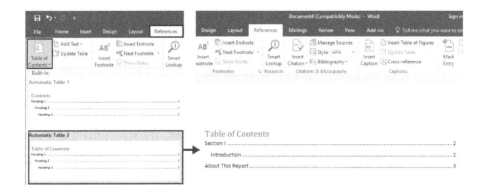

Note: Once additional sections and subsections are added to your document and you have applied Heading styles, to update your Table of Contents, click on the words *Table of Contents* (in your document), then click Update table, and select Update page numbers only, or Update entire table.

View Companion Video #14 to see these steps in action

Go to www.youtube.com and search for *#ezword14*

Part III: *Working With Tables*

Contents

Working With Tables

#15: How to Automatically Format Tables

To create a quick preformatted table:

1. From the Insert tab, click Table.
2. Hover over (or click) Quick Tables.
3. Built-in table styles include Calendar, Matrix, Tabular List, and Table with Subheads:

In this example, the Matrix style is selected and shown below. You can change the color scheme by selecting the up or down arrows in the Design tab:

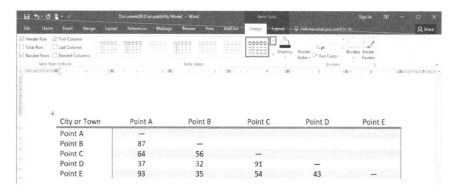

Hover over the new color scheme to see the result; or click to apply the new color scheme:

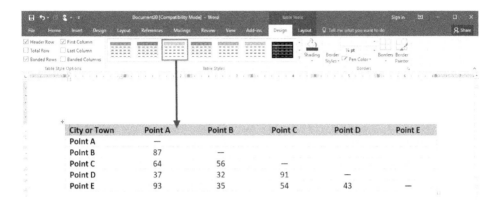

City or Town	Point A	Point B	Point C	Point D	Point E
Point A	—				
Point B	87	—			
Point C	64	56	—		
Point D	37	32	91	—	
Point E	93	35	54	43	—

Your preformatted table in the color of your choice is now ready for you to edit and fill in!

View Companion Video #15 to see these steps in action

Go to www.youtube.com and search for *#ezword15*

#16:   How to Repeat a Table Header Row

If your table exceeds one page, you will no longer see the column headings (Header Row) on subsequent pages. In this example, the Sales Receipt template is shown. Notice that the column headings are not shown on the second page:

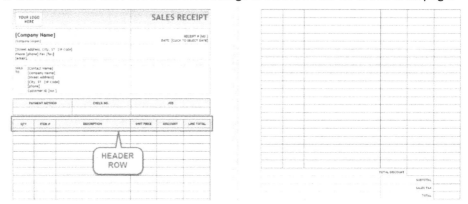

To have the top row (or rows) of a table repeat on other pages:

1. First, select the top row of the table. You may also select additional adjacent rows, but the selection must include the first row of the table.
2. In the Ribbon, under Table Tools, click the Layout tab.
3. Click Repeat Header Rows.

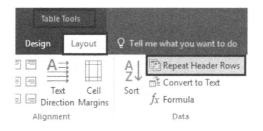

Here's the result:

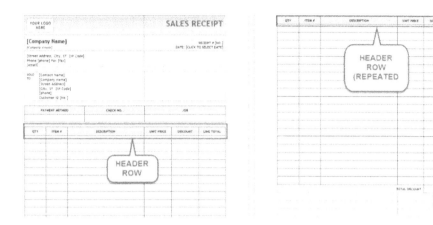

Note: You can only edit the header row(s) on the first page; on subsequent pages, the header row(s) are locked. If you change the header row on the first page, the heading changes on all other pages. Exception: if you insert a manual page break within a table, the header row(s) will not repeat.

View Companion Video #16 to see these steps in action

Go to www.youtube.com and search for *#ezword16*

To quickly resize a table:

1. First, hover over the table (or click in the table) until you see the little square images on the upper left and lower right of the table as shown here:

2. Position your mouse pointer on the bottom right of the table until you see a double-headed arrow as shown here:

3. Press and drag your mouse inward (to reduce) or outward (to enlarge) the entire table.

To change the width of a column:

1. Position the mouse pointer on the vertical line on the right side of the column until you see a vertical line with the double-header arrow as shown here:

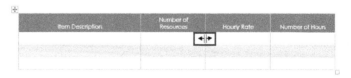

2. Press and drag your mouse to the left (to reduce) or to the right (to increase) the column width. The same procedures can be followed to alter the height of a row.

View Companion Video #17 to see these steps in action

Go to www.youtube.com and search for **#ezword17**

So, you've created a table and now it needs a tune up because some of the columns have changed. Some columns are too wide and some are too narrow. Many columns need about the same size width, so you need a quick way to distribute the columns evenly in your table. You also need to increase the row height to approximately double the current height. ***Here's how:***

First, select the rows or columns to resize. To select the whole table, hover over the table (or click inside the table), and click on the little square on the upper left, as shown here:

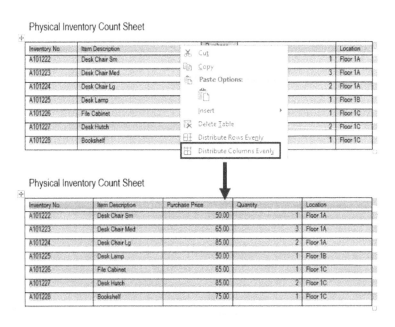

Right click in the selected area of the table, and click Distribute Columns Evenly.

Now that the columns are distributed evenly, you want the rows to also be distributed evenly, but you want to increase the row height. You can do this in one step by resizing the table (refer to the previous section entitled *Tables: How to Resize a Table* and dragging outward to increase the size of the table). Remember, all you need to do is position your mouse pointer on the bottom right of the table until you see a double-headed arrow, then press and drag outward, and voila!

Here's the result:

Physical Inventory Count Sheet

Inventory No.	Item Description	Purchase Price	Quantity	Location
A101222	Desk Chair Sm	50.00	1	Floor 1A
A101223	Desk Chair Med	65.00	3	Floor 1A
A101224	Desk Chair Lg	85.00	2	Floor 1A
A101225	Desk Lamp	50.00	1	Floor 1B
A101226	File Cabinet	65.00	1	Floor 1C
A101227	Desk Hutch	85.00	2	Floor 1C
A101228	Bookshelf	75.00	1	Floor 1C

Position your mouse pointer on the bottom right of table until you see the double-headed arrow: then press and drag to enlarge your table to desired size.

View Companion Video #18 to see these steps in action

Go to www.youtube.com and search for *#ezword18*

If you're on your way to work and pressed for time, would you take the long way filled with extra stop signs and traffic, or would you consider a shortcut that will get you there in less than half the time? Let's look at five ways to insert a row in a table, from slowest to fastest:

Method #1 (Insert a Row or Column via Ribbon): To insert a row or column from the Ribbon, first, click in your table (in the location you would like to insert). Tables Tools should now be visible in the Ribbon. From Table Tools, click the Layout tab; then in the Rows and Columns group, click the appropriate Insert command.

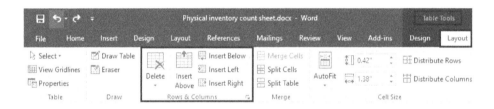

Method #2 (Insert a Row or Column via right-click menu): From inside a table, right-click in a table cell, click Insert, and click on the desired Insert command.

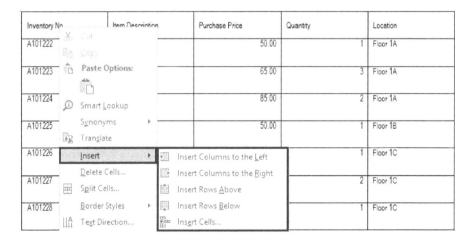

Method #3 (Insert a Row or Column in 1 Step - NEW! For Word 2016): Hover your mouse on the left outside edge of your table (in between the rows you would like to insert) until you see a circle with a plus sign; click the plus sign to instantly insert a row. To instantly insert a column, hover on the top outside edge of your table (in between the columns you would like to insert); click the plus sign in the circle to insert a column.

Method #4 (another nifty trick to quickly add a row!): Click at the end of the row above where you would like to insert a new row (outside the table on the right) and press ENTER. That's it! Presto...a new row is inserted below the current row:

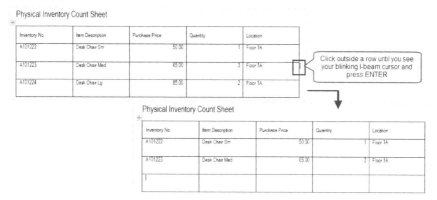

Method #5 (yet another way to insert a row at end of a table): Click in the last cell of your table on the bottom right. Then press TAB. Voila! A new row is inserted at the bottom of the table. The only exception for using this method is that it only works at the end of a table to insert a new row.

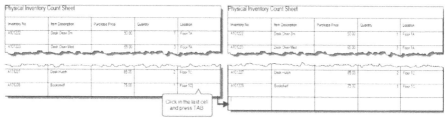

So, in conclusion, there are at least 5 ways to insert a row and 3 ways (so far) to insert a column. If you know another way, I'd love to hear from you!

View Companion Video #19 to see these steps in action

Go to www.youtube.com and search for *#ezword19*

#20: *Gridlines vs. Borders – What's the Difference?*

Gridlines are little dotted lines that show the cell boundaries of a table in areas where no borders have been applied. Unlike borders, gridlines appear only on the screen. They don't print, or appear in Print Preview or Web Layout view. In some case, gridlines are hidden (i.e. in some templates like the one shown below to the left).

To show gridlines, select your table; then from the Table Tools Ribbon, click Layout, View Gridlines. Here's the result:

Table borders are different from gridlines, because they display on your screen when using Print Preview and Web Layout view, and they print out as well. They can also enhance your table and make it easier to read the information in a table. ***Here's how to add borders to a table***:

First, select the table:

From the Home tab on the Ribbon, click on the drop-down menu and select a border style. Presto! Your table borders are applied. The All Borders option is selected below:

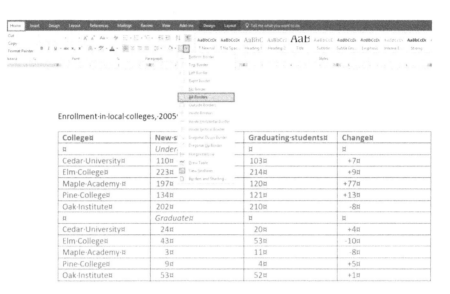

College¤	New·s	Graduating·students¤	Change¤
¤	*Under*	¤	¤
Cedar·University¤	110¤	103¤	+7¤
Elm·College¤	223¤	214¤	+9¤
Maple·Academy·¤	197¤	120¤	+77¤
Pine·College¤	134¤	121¤	+13¤
Oak·Institute¤	202¤	210¤	-8¤
¤	*Graduate¤*	¤	¤
Cedar·University¤	24¤	20¤	+4¤
Elm·College¤	43¤	53¤	-10¤
Maple·Academy·¤	3¤	11¤	-8¤
Pine·College¤	9¤	4¤	+5¤
Oak·Institute¤	53¤	52¤	+1¤

Enrollment·in·local·colleges,·2005'

View Companion Video #20 to see these steps in action

Go to www.youtube.com and search for *#ezword20*

Part IV: *The Document Screen*

Contents

#21:   *Setting Tabs Using the Ruler*

Word has a vertical and horizontal ruler which helps to align all kinds of things like text, graphics, tables and more. The horizontal ruler is especially handy for setting different types of tabs. To turn on, or *show* the rulers, from the View tab on the Ribbon, click the Ruler checkbox.

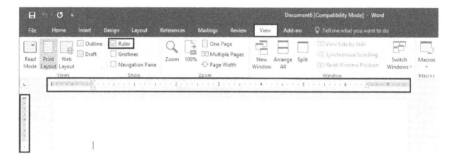

On the left of the horizontal ruler, there is a Tab Selector icon which shows an "L" in a small box, as shown below:

By default, there are left tabs set at every half inch. It's very easy to set new tabs.

Here's how:

1. Click the Tab Selector to select the type of tab you would like to set.
2. Click on the location on the ruler to set your new tab. Here are some examples of using the Left, Right and Decimal tabs:

Other helpful tab setting tips:

- To move your tab, just drag the existing tab to a new location on the ruler.
- To delete a tab, just drag it away from the ruler.
- When adding or changing any tabs, it will only affect selected text (or take effect starting at the current cursor position).
- Setting tabs via the horizontal ruler can save you lots of time vs. the traditional method using the Ribbon (Page Layout tab, Paragraph group, Tabs).

View Companion Video #21 to see these steps in action

Go to www.youtube.com and search for *#ezword21*

#22: *Splitting the Screen*

If you are working in a large document, the split screen feature allows you to view two different sections of the document at the same time.

To split the document screen:

From the Ribbon, click View, Split:

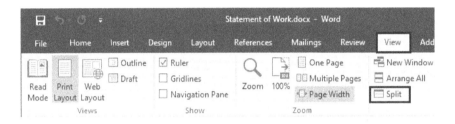

Your document window then splits into two sections, each with its own scroll bar. Click in the top or bottom pane to edit the desired section of the document.

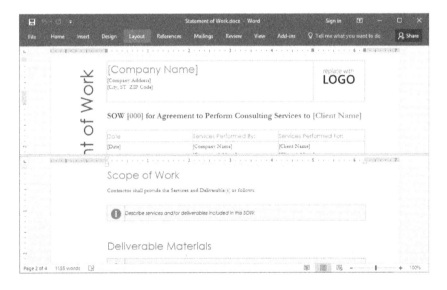

To remove the split screen:

From the Ribbon, click View, Remove Split (or just drag the horizontal line which is splitting your document up to the top of the document).

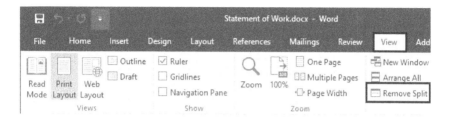

Note: In older versions of Word, another way to split your document screen is to drag the horizontal line (at the top of the vertical scroll bar) downward. The option is no longer available in Word 2013/2016.

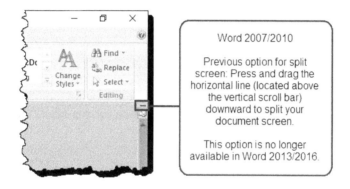

Beginning in Word 2013/2016, there are enhanced features in the View tab which allow you to view two documents side by side, with synchronous scrolling:

Here is an example of how you can view two documents side by side, with synchronous scrolling turned on:

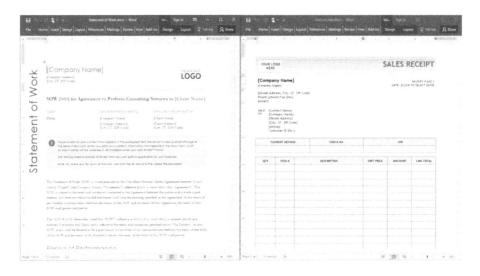

View Companion Video #22 to see these steps in action

Go to www.youtube.com and search for *#ezword22*

#23: *Turning the Ribbon On/Off*

If you need more real estate for your document, you may want to consider temporarily turning off the Ribbon. Newer versions of Word make it easier than ever to toggle Ribbon options off and on. In Word 2013/2016, you can automatically hide the ribbon (Auto-hide Ribbon), show the ribbon tabs only (Show tabs), or show both the ribbon and tabs (Show Tabs and Commands).

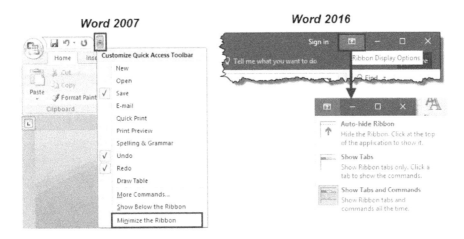

If you select Auto-hide Ribbon, a blue bar displays and the ribbon is hidden; hover over the blue bar to show/not show the Ribbon:

If you select Show Tabs, then only the tabs will display but not the Ribbon:

If you select Show Tabs and Commands, then both the tabs as well as the Ribbon display:

View Companion Video #23 to see these steps in action

Go to www.youtube.com and search for *#ezword23*

Part V: *Saving Options*

Contents

Saving Options

Saving a Document as a Template
Password Protecting a Document
Customizing Save Location

#24: *Saving a Document as a Template*

The mere act of saving and renaming your document does not convert it into an actual template. If you are copying and reusing documents over and over, consider saving your document as a template.

When saving a document as a template:

- the file extension changes from (.docx) to (.dotx).
- a master copy of your document is saved in a different location thereby preserving an original copy of your document, with no danger of the original file getting changed or edited.
- you can reuse the template as many times as you wish, and even delete all document versions, but the original copy is always saved in a safe place.
- you access the template via File, New.

To save your document as a template, with your document opened, do the following:

1. Click File, Save As.
2. Click Browse; then navigate to the destination folder.
3. In the Save As type drop-down, select Word Template (*.dotx).
4. Word automatically changes the destination path to the default Templates folder. The file extension is also automatically changed from .docx to .dotx in the File name field. Click Save.

To see the template in action, from a new blank document window, do the following:

1. Click File, New.
2. Featured Templates display by default. Click Personal to view any new templates you created.
3. Your Personal template(s) display.
4. Click on the desired template.
5. Your template displays in your document window. Edit as needed and then click File, Save As to save your completed document. This saves your document with the normal .docx file extension. Now each time you need to use your master template, you can easily find it via File, New, and clicking the Personal tab!

View Companion Video #24 to see these steps in action

Go to www.youtube.com and search for *#ezword24*

#25:   *Password Protecting a Document*

Whether you have important documents saved on your local hard drive, a network drive, or via an online storage service like Dropbox, if there's confidential information in your document, it's important to protect your files.

Consider password protecting your document. This will prevent people from opening or modifying your document.

Here's how:

1. Open your document. Click File, Protect Document, Encrypt Document. (Note: This step is the same in Word 2010; in Word 2007, click the Office Button, Prepare, Encrypt Document.)

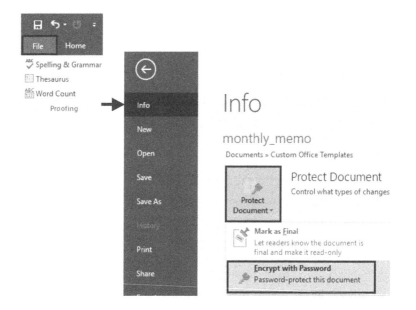

2. In the Encrypt Document dialog box, enter a password and click OK.

3. In the Confirm Password dialog box, re-enter the password and click OK.

Important Note: Microsoft Word cannot retrieve forgotten passwords, so be sure to use a password that's strong, yet easy for you to remember.

View Companion Video #25 to see these steps in action

Go to www.youtube.com and search for **#ezword25**

#26:   *Customizing Save Location*

When you save documents, where exactly do they go?

If you don't change a thing, Word decides where to store your documents. By default, Word will store your files in a folder called Documents, located on your local C: drive, which is referred to as This PC in your drive locations. But where exactly is the Documents folder? It's actually nested a few folders deep on your C: drive. Take a look:

> This PC > OS (C:) > Users > Amelia1 > Documents > samples

When you save a document, you can easily change the location of where you want to save your files by changing the default file location. ***Here's how:***

1. Click File, Options. (In Word 2010: click File, Word Options; in Word 2007, click the Office Button, Options.)
2. Click Save.
3. In the Default local file location field, click Browse, change to the preferred folder, and click OK.

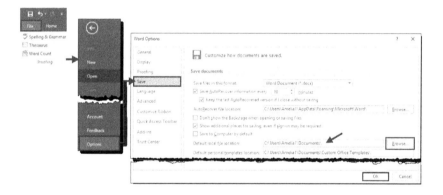

Now each time you save a document, your preferred file location will default. It will also default to the location to browse for files when you open documents as well.

Note: Another way to set up a preferred location to save or open files is to set up a Favorite. From the Save As dialog box (or Open dialog box), navigate to your preferred file location, right click on the folder, and click Pin to List. Your preferred file location is then added to your Pinned list:

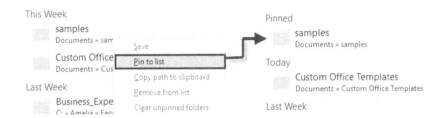

It's a little different depending on the version of Microsoft Word you are using. In Word 2010, right click on Favorites and click Add current location to Favorites; in Word 2007, right-click on Quick Access, and click Pin current folder to Quick access; the latter adds the file location to the Quick access list.

View Companion Video #26 to see these steps in action

Go to www.youtube.com and search for *#ezword26*

Part VI: *Getting Creative*

Contents

#27:   *How to Add a Page Border*

Let's get creative! Did you know you can add a plain or fancy border to one or more pages in a document? You can select a line style and change the width or color, or you can select an art border with a variety of graphics. You can also find additional borders in Microsoft Office templates. It's easy to apply borders and add a bit of flare to your document. Here are some sample borders:

Here's how:

In Word 2013/2016, select Design, Page Borders (in Word 2007/2010, select Page Layout, Page Borders). Then from the Page Border tab in the Borders and Shading dialog box, select the Setting (e.g. "Box"), Style (e.g. "Multiple line"), Color (e.g. "Blue"), Width (e.g. "3 pt"), Apply to (e.g. "This section – first page only"), click OK:

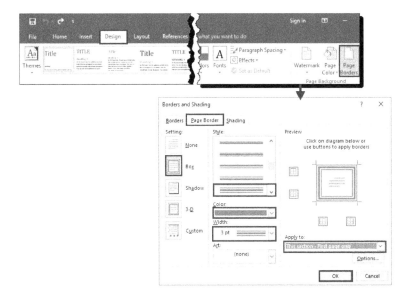

To select an art border, from the Page Border tab in the Borders and Shading dialog box, instead of selecting a line style, click in the Art drop down arrow and select from the wide range of fancy borders. If a black and white border is selected (second image below), you can select a color to replace or enhance the black/white default color).

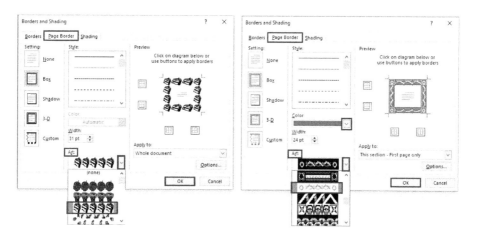

Note: You can find sample documents with borders in Microsoft Word templates by clicking File, New, and entering "borders" in the search box.

View Companion Video #27 to see these steps in action

Go to www.youtube.com and search for *#ezword27*

If you need to draw a horizontal line across the page, one way would be to use Insert, Shapes, Line, and manually draw a line. This gives you full control of the width, thickness and color of the line. However, there's a little secret trick that quickly lets you create several different types of lines with just a few keystrokes using your keyboard.

All you have to do is press a key three times and then press Enter. Different keys will give you different types of lines. ***Here's how:***

For a solid line across the page, press the Hyphen key three times and press Enter. Here's the result:

For a thicker line across the page, press the Underline key three times and press Enter. Here's the result:

For a broken line across the page, press the Asterisk key three times and press Enter. Here's the result:
■■■

For a double line across the page, press the Equal Sign three times and press Enter. Here's the result:

===

For a squiggly line across the page, press the Tilde key (Shift plus the key to the left of the "1" key), three times and press Enter. Here's the result:

∼∼

Note: Once these lines are drawn, they are a little tricky to delete, as there's no way to click and grab hold of them. However, here's all you have to do to remove them: Place the cursor below the line (on a hard return); then press Backspace. Presto! The line is gone as quickly as it appeared.

View Companion Video #28 to see these steps in action

Go to www.youtube.com and search for *#ezword28*

#29:   *Online Pictures*

Although you have always been able to insert pictures in Microsoft Word, there's a new feature in Word 2013/2016 which allows you to search and insert images from online sources without leaving your document window. *Here's how:*

From the Insert tab on the Ribbon, click Online Pictures:

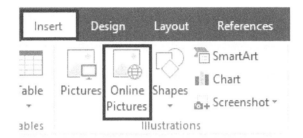

When the Insert Pictures dialog box displays, you will be prompted to log in to your Microsoft account. This allows you to insert photos and videos from OneDrive, Flickr, and other sites:

Once you have logged in to your Microsoft account, additional options display. You can search for images on Bing.com, on your OneDrive personal online storage, or by connecting to Flickr or Facebook. In this example, we'll use the Bing search box. Enter one or more search words in the search box. In this example, "umbrella" is entered in the search box. Then click Search (little magnifying glass icon).

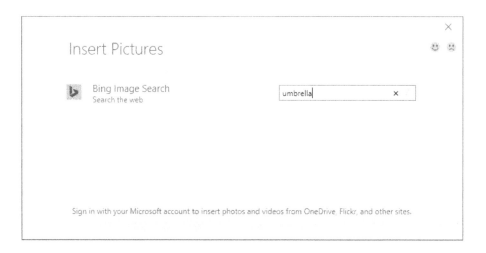

Images matching the search criteria are displayed. Be sure to review the Creative Commons licenses and comply. To insert an image, click the checkbox for the image, and click Insert.

Note: This option is not available in Word 2007 or 2010. Online Pictures first became available in Word 2013.

View Companion Video #29 to see these steps in action

Go to www.youtube.com and search for **#ezword29**

#30:   *Inserting Symbols*

There's a large array of symbols to use in Microsoft Word. You can insert symbols like Copyright ©, Trademark ®, smiley faces ☺, Infinity symbol∞ and even little pictures like this: ✉ ☎ ✈ ☀. To use symbols, click Insert, Symbol. Some commonly used symbols display. To view even more symbols to select from, click More Symbols:

From the Symbol dialog box, you can select from a variety of Fonts and Subsets to view more symbols. Change the font to Webdings and Wingdings to see the variety of graphical symbols available. To insert a symbol, click to select the symbol, and then click Insert.

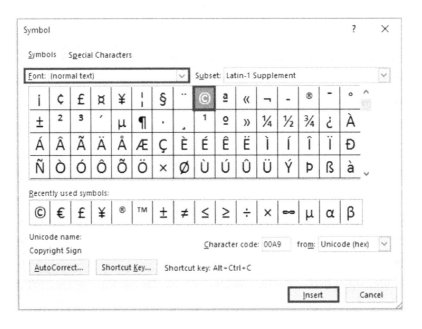

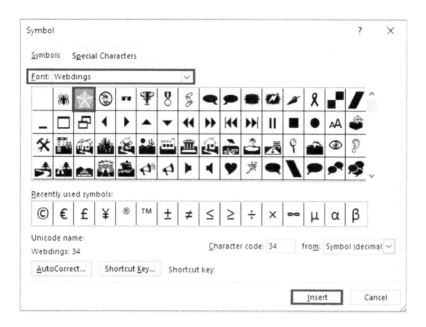

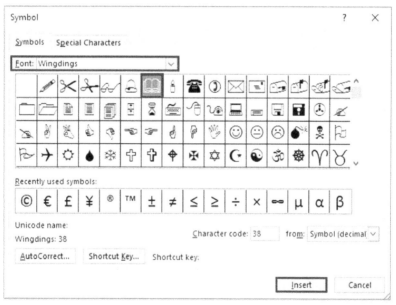

There are also keyboard shortcuts for lots of symbols. For example:

- To quickly insert the copyright symbol using your keyboard, type: (c) and the result is: ©.
- To quickly insert the trademark symbol using your keyboard, type (r) and the result is: ®.

Additional keyboard shortcuts can be found in AutoCorrect Options. Click File, Options (Word Options in Word 2007), Proofing, AutoCorrect Options. In the bottom portion of the AutoCorrect dialog box, notice the keystrokes on the left and the matching symbol on the right:

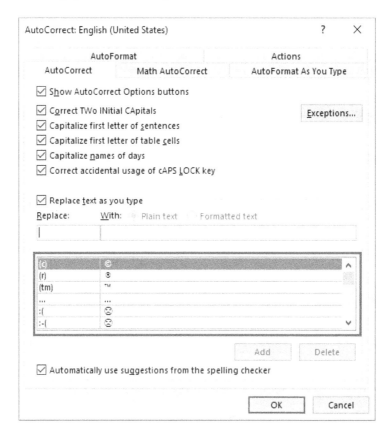

This includes the smiley face icons which are popular in social media. You can experiment with the keystrokes to quickly add the symbols of your choice.

View Companion Video #30 to see these steps in action

Go to www.youtube.com and search for *#ezword30*

Part VII: *Extras*

Contents

Extras

Keyboard and Mouse Shortcuts

- To go to the beginning of a line, press the Home key.
- To go to the end of a line, press the End key.
- If you want to quickly navigate to the very top of a document, press Ctrl + Home key.
- To move to the end of the document, press Ctrl + -End key.
- To undo the last operation, press Ctrl + Z.

Three ways to copy selected text (or graphics):

- CTRL+C
- CTRL+INSERT
- From the Ribbon, click the Copy icon in the Home tab.

Two ways to cut select text (or graphics):

- CTRL+X
- From the Ribbon, click the Cut icon in the Home tab.

Three ways to paste select text (or graphics):

- CTRL+V
- SHIFT+INSERT
- From the Ribbon, click the Paste icon in the Home tab.

View Companion Video #31 to see these steps in action

Go to www.youtube.com and search for ***#ezword31***

#32:   *Inserting Date and Time*

You can automatically insert the date and time in a variety of formats. **Here's how:**

1. Click Insert, Date and Time.
2. A variety of formats will display. Select a date format.
3. If you check the Update Automatically box, Word will insert a date field and update it automatically.
4. If you click the Set As Default button, it will set the selected format as your default selection.
5. When you're ready to insert the date and time, click OK.

View Companion Video #32 to see these steps in action

Go to www.youtube.com and search for **#ezword32**

#33:   How to Customize Initials in Comments

If you are sending a document to a team of individuals and they will be adding feedback and comments to your document, you may see some unrecognizable initials in the Comment box to the right like this:

To insert Comments, position the cursor to the desired location in the document, then click Insert, Comment. In this example, two individuals left comments. Reviewer #1 is AG1 and reviewer #2 is AR1.

To customize the initials which appear in Comments:

1.   Click File, Options (Word Options in Word 2007).
2.   In the General tab, edit the User name and Initials and click OK:

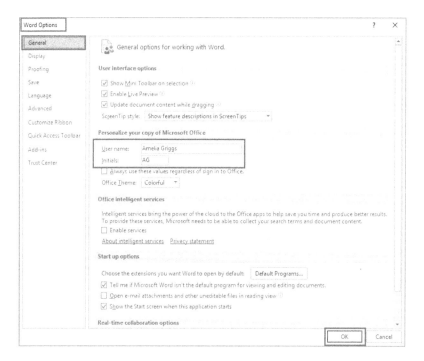

Once each reviewer changes his/her user name, this will be reflected in Comments. Here's the result:

Exception: If a user is logged in to their Microsoft Office account, the user name in Comments will default based on the Microsoft user account name.

View Companion Video #33 to see these steps in action

Go to www.youtube.com and search for *#ezword33*

#34:   Adding and Customizing a Page Number

You just typed a 3-page memo and you need to place the page number at bottom center; however, you want to omit the page number from the first page.

It's easy to insert and customize page numbers in Microsoft Word.

Here's how:

1. From the Insert tab of the Ribbon, click Page Number from the Header & Footer group:

2. The available page number locations and options display. In this example, to insert the page number at bottom center, select Bottom of Page, and then select the second option on the right to select the center position:

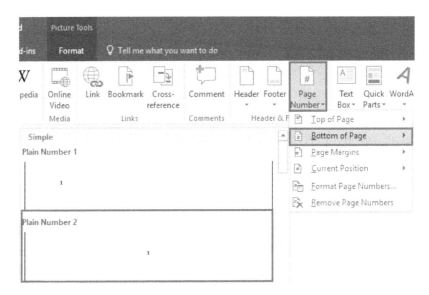

3. To omit the page number from the first page, double-click in the Footer area of your document (preferably, on the first page). The Header Footer options will then display in the Ribbon. Check the box for Different First Page. Finally, since you want to omit the page number from the first page, select the page number field (highlight it as shown below) and press Delete.

Your page number will now begin on page 2.

Note: To further customize your page number (for example, to create a custom format: **–Page 2–**), double click on the page number (in this case, at the bottom of page 2); then click before or after the page number, then enter your additional text.

View Companion Video #34 to see these steps in action

Go to www.youtube.com and search for **#ezword34**

For our final tip, let's discuss the Show/Hide. The Show/Hide can be found in the Home tab on the Ribbon.

- Click Show/Hide to show symbols.
- Click Show/Hide again to toggle off or hide symbols.

Have you noticed that when you hover (but don't click) over an icon on the Ribbon, a little tool tip displays beneath the icon in a little box? This is a quick way for you to get a brief description of any icon, including the Show/Hide.

You can click "? Tell me more" at the bottom of the tool tip box for more info.

Basically, the Show/Hide lets you see (shows) or not see (hides) paragraph marks and other formatting symbols in your document. Each space is shown as a dot. You might find it helpful to see these formatting symbols to confirm if you have one or two spaces after a period, or to check for hard return symbols when trying to delete a blank line.

Examples of formatting symbols:

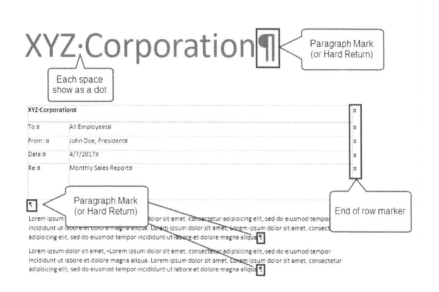

View Companion Video #35 to see these steps in action

Go to www.youtube.com and search for *#ezword35*

Many Thanks!

I hope you have enjoyed learning these tips, tricks, shortcuts, and a few little "secrets" in Microsoft Word.

Thank you for purchasing this book!

Want to see all the tips in action?

Visit Easylearningweb's youtube channel
http://www.youtube.com/user/easylearningweb for online training videos.

Want more tips, tricks and shortcuts?

Visit http://easylearningweb.com for the latest updates on new books, articles, videos and more!

Can I ask for a small favor? Could you please take a minute or two and leave a review on Amazon? Please visit http://www.amazon.com/feedback. Your review will help me improve content in future books. Thank you in advance for your feedback!

Other Books in the Series by Amelia Griggs:

(3 Book Series Available in 2018)

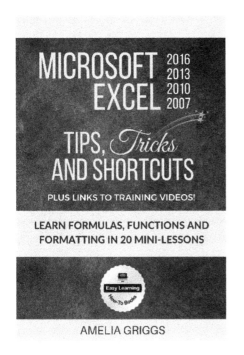 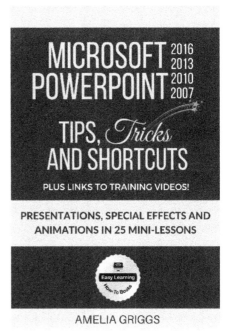

To be notified when new books and videos are available, get links to new blog articles and be alerted for book giveaways and free gifts, join the Easy Learning Newsletter:

http://eepurl.com/cNULVr

Don't miss out! Join Today!

www.ingramcontent.com/pod-product-compliance
Lightning Source LLC
LaVergne TN
LVHW080103070326
832902LV00014B/2390